AMAZING HOCKEY STORIES

CONNOR McDAVID

Lorna Schultz Nicholson

Illustrations by D. A. Bishop

Scholastic Canada Ltd.
Toronto New York London Auckland Sydney
Mexico City New Delhi Hong Kong Buenos Aires

With thanks to Connor, Kelly and Brian McDavid for their amazing help with stories and photos. — *L. S. N.*

Scholastic Canada Ltd.
604 King Street West, Toronto, Ontario M5V 1E1, Canada

Scholastic Inc.
557 Broadway, New York, NY 10012, USA

Scholastic Australia Pty Limited
PO Box 579, Gosford, NSW 2250, Australia

Scholastic New Zealand Limited
Private Bag 94407, Botany, Manukau 2163, New Zealand

Scholastic Children's Books
Euston House, 24 Eversholt Street, London NW1 1DB, UK

www.scholastic.ca

Library and Archives Canada Cataloguing in Publication
Schultz Nicholson, Lorna, author
Connor McDavid / Lorna Schultz Nicholson ; illustrated by
D.A. Bishop.

(Amazing hockey stories)
ISBN 978-1-4431-5778-0 (softcover)

1. McDavid, Connor, 1997- --Juvenile literature. 2. Edmonton
Oilers (Hockey team)--Juvenile literature. 3. Hockey players--Alberta--
Edmonton--Biography--Juvenile literature. I. Title.

GV848.5.M38S38 2017   j796.962092   C2017-901492-7

Photos ©: cover: Gregg Forwerck/NHLI/Getty Images; cover background and
throughout: Nik Merkulov/Shutterstock; 4: Ronald Martinez/Getty Images; 6:
Courtesy the McDavid Family; 8 left: Courtesy the McDavid Family; 8 right: Courtesy
the McDavid Family; 14: Courtesy the McDavid Family; 16: Courtesy the McDavid
Family; 18: Courtesy the McDavid Family; 20: Erie Otters; 23: Courtesy the McDavid
Family; 25: Matt Mead Photography LLC; 32: Dennis Pajot/Getty Images; 34: Dennis
Pajot/Getty Images; 36: Courtesy the McDavid Family; 41: Ronald Martinez/Getty
Images; 48: Jonathan Kozub/NHLI/Getty Images; 50: Andy Devlin/NHLI/Getty Images;
53: YURI KADOBNOV/AFP/Getty Images; 61: Codie McLachlan/Getty Images.

6 5 4 3 2 1   Printed in Canada 119   17 18 19 20 21

MIX
Paper from
responsible sources
FSC® C103113

CONTENTS

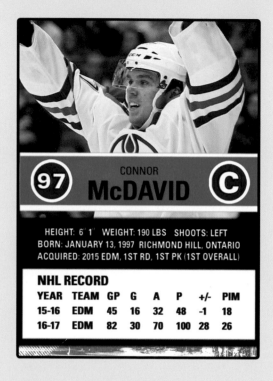

CONNOR
McDAVID
97 C

HEIGHT: 6' 1' WEIGHT: 190 LBS SHOOTS: LEFT
BORN: JANUARY 13, 1997 RICHMOND HILL, ONTARIO
ACQUIRED: 2015 EDM, 1ST RD, 1ST PK (1ST OVERALL)

NHL RECORD

YEAR	TEAM	GP	G	A	P	+/-	PIM
15-16	EDM	45	16	32	48	-1	18
16-17	EDM	82	30	70	100	28	26

On October 5, 2016, at the age of 19 years and 266 days, Connor McDavid became the Edmonton Oilers' 15th captain and the youngest captain in the history of the NHL.

Wearing the "C" on his jersey, he stepped on the ice and wowed fans with two goals and an assist in the first game of the season, against the Calgary Flames.

Connor's explosive skating, instinctive puck handling and crisp tape-to-tape passes make him a threat with the puck. His long strides and fast foot movement propel him around other players as if he has an extra gear. And, like a race car, he can shift into that high gear in a split second. He skates as fast with the puck as without it — something not many players can do.

Connor scores goals and makes brilliant plays. Whether it's behind the net, off to the side or at the hash marks, he can see a play that *might* be possible, and then he makes it happen. Nothing is more important than helping his team succeed.

He's a natural-born captain, no matter what his age, but Connor has also put in the hard work to achieve his dreams. As a kid, he spent all his free time shooting pucks, skating and perfecting moves he saw professional players doing. Not everything came easy for him either. He usually played with older players and sometimes the age difference was hard for him. The pressure was great. But he kept pushing forward.

Even today, Connor still likes to be the first one on the ice at practice and the last one off. He stays fit in his off-season. And he still shoots pucks, lots of pucks.

Some people think Connor McDavid was born with extraordinary skills. But, as he likes to say, he got his talent "from extraordinary hard work."

EARLY DAYS

CONNOR'S FIRST HOCKEY CARD, WITH THE AURORA MINOR HOCKEY ASSOCIATION. HIS MOTHER TOLD HIM TO "SMILE LIKE HE JUST WON THE STANLEY CUP."

When Connor was just three years old, he asked his mother to sew a "C" on his T-shirts. At first she thought it was because his name started with C, but then he told her it was because all the good hockey players on television had a "C" on their jerseys, and he wanted one too. Together they cut out little Cs, and his mother sewed them on his shirts. Maybe he was predicting his future.

THE MINI-ME

Connor loved going to the arena to watch his older brother, Cameron, play. Their father was one of the coaches for Cameron's team, so it was a family event for Connor. Cameron was four years older and called Connor "mini-me." When Cameron was eight, he played on a select team where he wore dress pants and a nice shirt and jacket for game days. And four-year-old Connor did too, showing up in a matching tie and hat and a hand-me-down team jacket. The team thought Cam's mini-me was a cool little guy and let him be the "assistant trainer." He filled water bottles and quietly listened to the coach's pre-game talks.

Once the game started, he sat in the stands with his mother, closely watching the action. And he was catching a lot more than people expected. When the other kids' parents missed what was going on, Connor piped up and gave them a play-by-play. He even understood the coach's strategy.

Connor had started skating when he was two. Right from those early days, being on the ice made Connor feel free. He loved the feeling of gliding and of moving fast. He also played rollerblade hockey games in his garage, using paint cans as opponents and stuffed animals as fans. After two years of public skating and playing hockey in his garage, four-year-old Connor had started bugging his parents to put him in real hockey. But his mother told him the rules said he had to be five.

"Pleeeeease," Connor begged, again and again and again.

(LEFT) CHRISTMAS 2003: BIG BROTHER CAMERON AND HIS "MINI-ME" CONNOR WEAR MATCHING JERSEYS.
(RIGHT) CHRISTMAS 2005: THE BROTHERS WITH A NEW JERSEY (CONNOR) AND HELMET (CAMERON).

THE LITTLE WHITE LIE

Although he wasn't old enough, Connor's parents gave in. He was driving them crazy! Connor's mother filled out the registration form for minor hockey, putting Connor's birth year as 1996 instead of 1997. She told him that if the association asked for his birth certificate, like they had with Cameron, he wouldn't be able to play. But luckily for Connor, no one asked! So, that September, when he was only four years old, Connor started playing house league hockey for Newmarket.

Connor quickly became the best player on his team and spent two years playing with Newmarket. He loved the challenge of playing with older players, he was ready for that. But it wasn't always easy being the youngest *and* one of the best, and sometimes he worried he didn't fit in.

PLAYING UP . . . AND UP

When it was time for Connor to move up to the next level, his parents felt so guilty for lying about his age that his father confessed. He told the association Connor's real birthday. But then they said Connor would have to play house league for *another* year with kids his *own* age. His father argued. He said that if kids were good at school they were allowed to move up a grade. Why not in hockey? It became apparent that Connor would have to change associations to play up a division.

CONNOR PLAYING FOR THE YORK SIMCOE EXPRESS. EVEN AT AN EARLY AGE, HE HAD EXCELLENT EDGE CONTROL AT FAST SPEEDS.

So Connor moved organizations and played for Aurora, and again he was the youngest player on the team. Sometimes it was hard for Connor because his teammates counted on him to score, and although he got a lot of goals, he didn't get one every single time!

When Connor was feeling stressed or sad about anything, he didn't lash out or have temper tantrums. He just didn't talk very much. Sometimes on the way home in the car after a hard game, he didn't say a single word. His parents kept asking him if he liked playing with older boys and he said he did. All he ever wanted to do was play hockey and play it well, even though there was a lot of pressure and he didn't always fit in.

When it came time for AAA hockey, Connor had to move again, to an association that had the advanced hockey he needed. He went to play with the York Simcoe Express AAA in the Ontario Minor Hockey Association. Again, he was the youngest on the team — but this time his dad was his coach! Connor still says that his dad is his favourite coach from his days in minor hockey.

Connor went on to play for York Simcoe for four years, leading his peewee AAA team to a gold medal at Ontario provincials. Connor also won a silver medal with York Simcoe at the famous Quebec International Pee-Wee Hockey Tournament.

CONNOR AND HIS PARENTS AFTER THE YORK SIMCOE EXPRESS WON THE 2009 ONTARIO PEEWEE CHAMPIONSHIP.

ANOTHER MOVE

Even though Connor liked having his father as his coach, it soon became time for another big move. Connor needed to learn other skills in a different way. His family explored the idea of him playing for the Toronto Marlboros of the Greater Toronto Hockey League.

The York Simcoe Express were very sad to let him go — Connor was the star of the team. It wasn't hard for him to score four goals a game, or to pick up six points in two playoff games. But success wasn't Connor's objective. He wanted to skate against even faster players and improve his skills.

To play in the GTHL, Connor had to go to school in Toronto — and this time he needed to follow the rules. Fortunately Connor's grandparents lived in Toronto, so Connor and his dad went to live with them. But it was hard for 13-year-old Connor to be away from the rest of his family. He missed his mom and his big brother, Cameron.

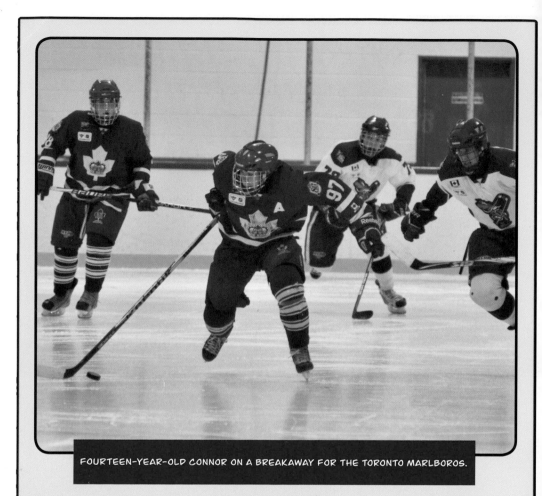

FOURTEEN-YEAR-OLD CONNOR ON A BREAKAWAY FOR THE TORONTO MARLBOROS.

Four months into Connor's first year as a bantam player, he got pulled up to play minor midget AAA. Most players in minor midget are 15 or 16, and Connor had just turned 14 in January, but he held his own. In just 33 games with his new team, he scored 27 goals and racked up 50 assists for 77 points — more than 2.3 points per game!

The following season he did even better. In 88 games he had 79 goals and 130 assists for a total of 209 points! Connor was named GTHL Player of the Year for the 2011–2012 season.

Connor wanted to get even better. The next level up was the Ontario Hockey League, but players are considered ineligible until they are 16 years old. So Connor did some research and found out that in the past, Hockey Canada had granted "exceptional player status" to John Tavares and Aaron Ekblad so they could play at the age of 15. The decision is based on several factors, including on-ice ability, academics and maturity. Connor wanted to apply for this. He said to his parents, "I have to do this."

"WHEN I WAS GROWING UP I WAS DIFFERENT. I WAS THE "WEIRD" KID ON ROLLERBLADES, BUT FOR ME IT WAS FUN. JUST KNOW IT'S OK TO BE DIFFERENT."
-- CONNOR McDAVID

THE ERIE OTTERS

OTTERS GENERAL MANAGER SHERRY BASSIN, CONNOR McDAVID AND CONNOR'S DAD, BRIAN McDAVID, SIGN CONNOR'S OHL CONTRACT IN APRIL 2012.

Hockey Canada granted Connor's request for exceptional player status. The Erie Otters were keen to get the hot young player. They had won only 10 of the 68 games they played in the 2011–2012 season, losing 52 in regulation time. Connor was selected as first pick in the 2012 OHL Priority Selection draft, and off he went to Erie, Pennsylvania.

He billeted with a family there, and went to high school. The rest of his teammates were 16 or older, so they were in a different part of the school. Connor was the lone Erie Otter over on the "other" side, where the younger kids went. He didn't know anyone, and at first he walked down the halls of his new school alone. He was homesick, but he knew the move was necessary to become a better player.

OHL ROOKIE

Connor didn't score in his first game with Erie but there was no stopping him after that. He had a point in 15 consecutive games and was named Rookie of the Month for both October and November. In Connor's first year in the OHL, he recorded 25 goals and 41 assists for a total of 66 points in 63 games.

The Otters played their final game on March 16, 2013, against the Guelph Storm. Connor nabbed four assists in that game, the most ever for an Erie Otters rookie. Connor was awarded the 2012–2013 Emms Family Award as the top rookie in the OHL, was a finalist for the CHL Rookie of the Year Award and was named to the OHL First All-Rookie Team.

Although all the awards and trophies were nice, Connor wanted something else. He wanted to make the playoffs! Even more, he wanted to feel that rush of playing for the Memorial Cup. The Otters finished their season with 19 wins, 40 losses and 4 overtime losses. With Connor the team had improved, but not quite enough to earn a playoff spot.

But there was a silver lining to not making the playoffs. Hockey Canada asked Connor to play in the 2013 IIHF U18 World Championship, which was taking place in Sochi, Russia. He jumped at the chance. Connor was the youngest player on the team *again*. He got off to a good start in the first game, against Slovakia, scoring a goal and tallying two assists. Against Sweden he scored a hat trick and was named the Canadian player of the game. When the final buzzer sounded in the championship game, the Canadians had won the gold medal, defeating Team USA. Connor, the scoring leader for the entire tournament, won tournament MVP and the award for best forward.

ON AND OFF THE ICE

All summer long Connor worked to stay fit. He ran hills, always trying to better his time on the way up. He spent a lot of time at the gym, riding the bike, lifting weights and doing lots of work with the medicine ball and chin-up bar. When September arrived he stepped back on the ice determined to bring a championship to his team. Game by game the Otters improved. Game by game Connor kept scoring and making plays.

That Christmas Connor made the 2014 World Junior hockey team. At 16, he was the youngest player on the team. The tournament didn't exactly go the way the Canadian fans had hoped. The lineup featured Ryan Nugent-Hopkins as captain, and the rest of the players were an all-star cast. On a team with some of the best 19-year-olds in the country, Connor didn't see too much ice. But the fourth-place finish was still tough to take.

CONNOR'S TALENT AND TEAM SPIRIT QUICKLY CAUGHT THE ATTENTION OF THE OTTERS' FANS.

For the rest of the 2013–2014 OHL season, Connor gritted his teeth and played serious hockey. He racked up points. By the end of the season, Connor had managed to get 28 goals and 71 assists for a total of 99 points in 56 games. The now 17-year-old had placed fourth overall in OHL scoring.

And the Otters made the playoffs! They had gone from winning only 19 games the season before to winning a healthy 52 games, putting them second overall in the OHL, with their young hotshot leading the way.

Connor loved the adrenalin and the fast pace of the playoffs. In 14 OHL playoff games, he scored 4 goals and added 15 assists for 19 points. But in the Western Conference final, the Erie Otters were defeated by the eventual OHL champions, the Guelph Storm.

Once again the trophies piled up at the end of the season, with a few new and important ones. Along with the William Hanley Trophy for most sportsmanlike player, Connor won the Bobby Smith Trophy for OHL scholastic player of the year and the CHL Scholastic Player of the Year Award. On top of the points, he was getting good grades! Connor was focused on his NHL dream, but he worked hard at school too.

YOUNG CAPTAIN CONNOR

At the beginning of the 2014–2015 season, Connor McDavid was named the captain of the Erie Otters. This was a role he was ready for. Two years with the Otters had given him the confidence he needed, and by Christmas the team was smoothly on track to make the playoffs. The 2015 World Junior Championships were on the horizon, and that year they were in Toronto — his former home with the Marlboros. But because of a single bad moment, Connor's chance at playing in them was in jeopardy.

CONNOR GOT THE "C" FOR THE 2014–2015 SEASON. COACH KRIS KNOBLAUCH SAID, "CONNOR WAS THE LEADER OF THE TEAM, WHO GUYS LOOKED UP TO."

BACK TO WORK

After winning gold with Team Canada and being named to the World Juniors All-Star Team, Connor returned to the Erie Otters. He was proud of his medal and of Canada (especially for beating Russia in the final), because Team Canada hadn't won the gold since 2009. And it had been awesome to win on home ice in Toronto.

But now, Connor needed to get back to work as captain of the Otters. He wanted his team to play in the Memorial Cup Tournament. Could they make it all the way?

PLAYOFF DREAMS

The Erie Otters finished their season with 50 wins and 18 losses, earning a berth in the playoffs. On March 26, 2015, they hit the ice, pumped with adrenalin to face off against the Sarnia Sting. But that adrenalin wasn't enough. Every time Connor had the puck he was checked. Over and over again. At the end of the game he was scoreless. They lost that first playoff game on home ice, 3–2. Connor headed to the dressing room, his head muddled with thoughts.

How could he get around the checks? What did his team have to do? What did *he* have to do to score? All night he thought about what they needed to do to win. The next day he talked to his team in the dressing room and told them they'd come a long way and improved and that they could win. He and his teammates talked about how they needed to look for plays, be patient and not turn over the puck.

When the Otters stepped on the ice on March 27, the fans cheered. Connor played crafty hockey, dodging his opponents, finding open ice and skating to the net. The first red light of the night went on for the Otters. But the goal judge had been too excited — the puck wasn't in the net. The refs called it back. This fired Connor up and he sunk one into Sarnia's net in the second period. The final score: 3–1 for the Erie Otters.

In the third game, the score was tied 5–5 in the third period. Connor found a loose puck and stick-handled through traffic, sending it to the back of the net for a game-winner!

The final game in the series ended up being a 7–0 blowout for Erie, and Connor had his first three-point game of the playoffs, scoring one goal and two helpers. Erie was moving on to face the London Knights in the semifinals.

THOUGH CONNOR IS OFTEN COMPARED TO WAYNE GRETZKY AND SIDNEY CROSBY, HE HAS TRIED NOT TO LET THE PRESSURE GET TO HIM.

Connor played good strategic hockey in their first game against the Knights. When the Otters got a five-minute penalty, Connor didn't let it shake him. Instead he wheeled down the ice and scored a short-handed goal. The score ended up 5–2 for the Otters, and Connor came away with two goals and four points. The Otters won their second game 7–3. Five of those seven goals belonged to Connor, a franchise playoff record.

In the third game of the series, Connor racked up three assists and was named CHL Player of the Week.

Although the Knights held Connor to two points in the fourth and final game of the series, he still came away with another franchise record: eight goals and fourteen points in a single series. Connor felt great about this series. He remembered playing in the London Arena when he was in his first season with the Otters. Back then his team just hoped they could get 10 shots on net! They'd come a long way.

ALMOST THERE

Next up: the Western Conference finals. It was the Erie Otters against the Sault Ste. Marie Greyhounds. In the first game the Soo took an early 3–0 lead. Connor responded — with a hat trick! But even with that hat trick, the Otters lost the battle 6–3.

The media was all over Connor after the game. The Hounds' style "is to come out hard and ramp up the intensity," he said. "They blitzed us early, but we bounced back."

In the second game, the Otters beat the Greyhounds on Sault Ste. Marie's home ice, where they hadn't lost in almost four months. Connor's first goal of the game and fourth of the series was 23 seconds into the third period. His second goal was on an empty net with 29.3 seconds left on the clock.

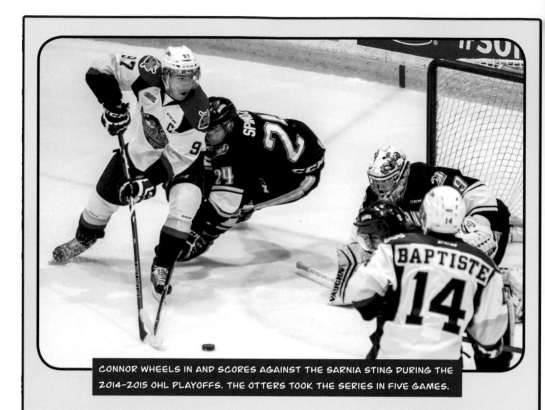

CONNOR WHEELS IN AND SCORES AGAINST THE SARNIA STING DURING THE 2014–2015 OHL PLAYOFFS. THE OTTERS TOOK THE SERIES IN FIVE GAMES.

In game three, Connor scored two goals. One was a short-handed beauty that made TV highlight reels all across North America. In game six, Connor also made four assists, with the Otters taking the game. But in game five, the Greyhounds hung on with a 4–2 win to make the series 2–2. In game six, the Otters took it, 7–3. Connor had a five-point night with a goal and four assists. The Erie Otters were going to the OHL finals, meeting up with the Oshawa Generals. The winner would go on to play for the Memorial Cup.

BITTERSWEET

Unfortunately, in a devastating defeat, the Erie Otters lost to the Generals four games to one. This was a huge disappointment for Connor and his team. Although Connor finished his last OHL season as the playoffs' leading scorer, with 21 goals and 28 assists for 49 points, the loss was painful. He wasn't able to achieve his dream of leading the Otters to a Memorial Cup win.

Connor said the dressing room afterward was quiet. "No one talked for a long time. We just sat there, crying, all choked up." When the Erie Otters got on their bus after the loss, "We hugged each other. And thanked each other. And we were happy to go home."

Connor knew that was the last game he would play with his Erie friends, but they celebrated at the CHL year-end banquet. The awards piled up for Connor again. He won the Player of the Year Award, was named top prospect and once again proudly took home the Scholastic Player of the Year Award. After the banquet, Connor was modest about his accomplishments, saying, "You come in as a 15-year-old just hoping to do the best you can, and for this to happen is very special."

The season was over, the scouting combine and 2015 NHL Entry Draft were coming up, and Connor had the summer ahead to train — and worry. Everyone was writing about him and projecting that he would be the first overall draft pick but Connor wasn't so sure. Would he actually play in the NHL or would he go to an AHL farm team? Was he going to be a Toronto Maple Leaf? Or a Buffalo Sabre? Or even an Edmonton Oiler?

CONNOR AT THE 2014–2015 OHL AWARDS CEREMONY AT THE HOCKEY HALL OF FAME IN TORONTO. HE WON THE RED TILSON TROPHY FOR MOST OUTSTANDING PLAYER AND THE BOBBY SMITH TROPHY FOR SCHOLASTIC PLAYER OF THE YEAR.

LIVING THE NHL DREAM

On June 26, 2015, at the BB&T Center in Sunrise, Florida, Connor sat in the stands with over 40 of his relatives. Some of them he'd never even met before, but they'd all come to watch the NHL Entry Draft. Connor's legs jiggled nervously and he felt queasy. The media thought either he or Jack Eichel would go first.

The Oilers had the first overall pick. Connor had already visited Edmonton with his parents, talked to people from the team and saw the plans for the new arena they were building. But what if they changed their minds? In front of flashing cameras, the Oilers' general manager, Peter Chiarelli, called Connor's name. He breathed a sigh of relief. The stress and uncertainty was over. But new pressures were about to begin.

GO WEST

Reality sunk in quickly — he would be moving again, even farther away from his family. Would it be weird to bring his Toronto Maple Leafs memorabilia from his old room? Of course it would. He was an Edmonton Oiler now. His parents wanted him to live with a family, like he'd done in Erie, but Connor wanted a change. When he arrived in Edmonton in August, he moved in with teammates Taylor Hall and Luke Gazdic. They were both older than he was — but that was something he was used to.

Connor settled in and took on the role of little brother. The Oilers' main camp went well and he skated hard. Connor was fast, could shoot the puck and score on NHL goalies. The coaches talked to him: they wanted him to jump from the OHL to the NHL at the age of 18.

So much was happening so fast! Connor was always in the media. People bought Oilers jerseys with his name on the back, and he hadn't even played a game yet. Fans showed up at *main camp* to watch him! Some people expected the young player to singlehandedly save the team.

Before he hit the ice for his first NHL game, Connor travelled to Penticton, British Columbia, to play in the Young Stars Tournament with the other prospects from the Oilers, Flames, Jets and Canucks. Fans in Penticton bought tickets for *all of* the Oilers games, hoping to get a glimpse of the Oilers' young star . . . but the coaches only put him in a single game. They were worried that other players might slam Connor into the boards, to try to injure him on purpose so he couldn't play. This was a great disappointment for many fans, but they wouldn't have wait too long to see him play.

THE JITTERS

The Oilers' NHL season started on the road on October 8, 2015 against the St. Louis Blues in Missouri. Connor sat in the dressing room. His hands were soaked with sweat. He felt sick with nerves. His legs shook. He held his stick tightly. The St. Louis Blues were a strong NHL team — even this early in the season they were considered Stanley Cup contenders. They had big men on their team, tougher than Connor had played against before. Connor stepped on the ice and played hard, feeling his way through this big man's game. He didn't score or even get a point. "Good not great" was how the newspapers described his debut.

After the game Connor said, "I did some good stuff, did some bad stuff." In his head he was analyzing his game. He knew what he had done well. In the third period, he had blown by Blues defenceman Jay Bouwmeester and skipped around defenceman Alex Pietrangelo to get a good shot on net — one that was a potential scoring chance. "I had a couple of chances that I need to score on," he said. But he wasn't happy with his faceoffs. After losing the first six, he had managed to win three of the next seven. But that wasn't good enough, and Connor knew he had to work harder.

Connor's second NHL game was on October 10 in Nashville, against the Predators, another strong team. Again, he didn't score but he played hard. After the game, Todd McLellan, the head coach of the Edmonton Oilers, talked to Connor. "Relax your hands on your stick," he said. "It'll come."

PICKING UP SPEED

Thankfully Connor had one more away game, against the Dallas Stars, to figure things out before having to play in front of the home crowd. Around the halfway mark of the second period, Connor saw Andrej Sekera shoot, and he also saw the potential for a tip. When Connor's stick hit that puck, it flew into the net from his backhand and he raised his arms in joy. Both arms and one leg. He'd scored his first NHL goal! After that goal, the media compared him to Sidney Crosby and Wayne Gretzky, who had also scored their first NHL goals in their third games.

CONNOR AFTER SCORING HIS FIRST NHL GOAL, AGAINST THE DALLAS STARS, IN THE SECOND PERIOD ON OCTOBER 13, 2015, IN DALLAS, TEXAS.

"I was excited but a lot of it was relief," said Connor. His entire body felt lighter — like something had been lifted off his back. "It's just the pressure out there these days. It felt good."

The Oilers' first home game was on October 15, 2015. This was to be the last home opener at Rexall Place — construction on the new Rogers Place arena was already underway.

When Connor stepped on the ice, he knew his family was in the stands. Fans had lined up for an hour and a half before the game. Cameras were everywhere. The demand for McDavid jerseys was incredible — unlike anything in years.

In the dressing room, Connor felt a little more confident than at his previous games. He had scored in Dallas. His hands felt looser on his stick. He could breathe better. But the game was a disappointment. The Oilers dropped a 4–2 loss to St. Louis, and Connor didn't even get a shot on net. He felt his play had not been good enough. And the next game was in two days, in Calgary — the Battle of Alberta.

WHO IS CONNOR'S FAVOURITE SUPERHERO?

BATMAN!

IN THE SPOTLIGHT

The Battle of Alberta was Connor's breakout game, with two goals and an assist. Next, the Oilers played the Canucks in Vancouver. Connor assisted on the opening goal, proving the Calgary game hadn't been a fluke.

The media attention on the young star was intense. He had to get used to the between-period interviews for television, especially during the *Hockey Night in Canada* games. With his helmet off, the sweat dripped down his face from the heat of the lights. He had to quickly switch from having his head in the game to talking to a reporter. And Connor didn't want to talk about himself, so he always tried to talk about his team.

The beginning of his NHL journey felt surreal to Connor. He was actually playing iconic teams in historic arenas! When the Oilers met the Detroit Red Wings in his seventh game, on October 21 at Rexall Place, Connor was pumped. Early in the second period, he rushed down the ice with his teammate Mark Letestu. It was two-on-one and short-handed to boot. Letestu didn't score, but the Oilers killed off the penalty and Connor was on fire. At 6:34 in the second period, Benoit Pouliot passed him the puck in a two-on-one rush. And in Connor fashion, he buried it. This became a highlight-reel goal, and his fourth goal of the season. The Oilers won that game 3–1.

BY THE TIME THE 2016 TIM HORTONS HERITAGE CLASSIC CAME AROUND, CONNOR HAD BECOME CONFIDENT WITH GAME-TIME INTERVIEWS.

COLLARBONE CRASH

Game after game, Connor played against stars he had only ever watched on TV. And coming up on November 6, he would play against his hero: Sidney Crosby.

The Philadelphia Flyers were in Edmonton on November 3. Near the end of the second period, as he lined up for a faceoff, Connor looked up at the clock. It was 2–1 for Philly, with only two minutes left in the period. A goal would give his team momentum.

When he got the puck on his stick, he moved fast toward the net. He saw an opening. Flying at full speed . . . he caught an edge. His body flew, fell and slid, slamming into the boards. Pain shot through his shoulder. He got up and headed to the bench, holding his arm. Glancing up, he saw there was only 1:44 left before the buzzer.

Wincing, Connor sat on the end of the bench. He shook his head when trainers asked him if he wanted to go the dressing room. As he watched, the pain intensified and his face paled. The buzzer finally sounded and Connor tried to stand. His legs wobbled and he almost threw up. A trainer grabbed him and guided him to the dressing room.

The team doctor assessed his injury. Broken collar bone. Connor would have to sit out for three months! He'd only played 13 games. His heart sank.

Suddenly his NHL life changed speed. He stayed back when the team travelled. The condo was quiet and lonely, and he watched Oilers away games from his sofa. The TV games were hard for him to watch. He felt responsible when the team lost — he wasn't there to help — and when they won he wasn't there to celebrate with them. For home games he dressed in a suit and sat upstairs with management and other teammates who were unable to play.

This would be the first Christmas since he was little that he didn't play — he'd always been in holiday tournaments. But he didn't take a break. Connor couldn't wait to get back on the ice. He rode his exercise bike constantly, and as soon as the sling came off, he did upper-body workouts. Doctors and coaches told him to be patient.

Finally, on February 1, after the All-Star break, Connor was cleared to play. His team had won only 14 of 37 games in his absence. When Connor stepped on the ice to play the Columbus Blue Jackets the next night, fans hung over the boards trying to get a glimpse of his big return. Sports reporters talked about him. Cameras flashed.

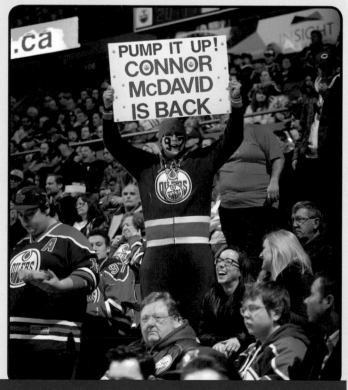

CONNOR WASN'T THE ONLY ONE WHO WAS HAPPY WHEN HE WAS GIVEN THE GREEN LIGHT TO PLAY AGAIN AFTER BREAKING HIS COLLARBONE.

BACK ON TRACK

Connor charged down the ice on the first faceoff and drew a penalty. Not a bad start. But the best was yet to come. Halfway through, the game was tied. Connor had the puck at centre ice. Then, as if he had turbos on his skates, he accelerated in a few short strides, splitting the defence and leaving them with their jaws dropped. Deking out the goalie, he fired the puck into the back of the net. Rexall Place exploded in cheers. Instead of his usual one-leg-up goal celebration, Connor fell to his knees and slid across the ice, pumping his fist in the air three times.

There had been countless five-point games in Connor's minor and junior hockey career. On February 11, 2016, he had his first five-point NHL game, against the Toronto Maple Leafs. This was a big deal to him. Coming from Newmarket, Ontario, Connor grew up watching the Leafs play.

Unfortunately, the Edmonton Oilers didn't make the playoffs that year. They finished with 31 wins, 43 losses and 8 overtime losses, for a total of 70 points. Still, this was an eight-point improvement over how the Oilers had done the year before. In Connor's first NHL season, he had scored 16 goals and had 32 assists for a grand total of 48 points in 45 games. He finished fourth among all rookies in scoring, even after missing three months of the season, and was nominated for the Calder Memorial Trophy for NHL Rookie of the Year. He didn't win it, but after losing so much time with his broken collarbone, it was a feat just to be nominated.

INTERNATIONAL UPS AND DOWNS

In the spring of 2016 Connor won another gold medal playing for Team Canada at the World Championships in Russia. Then in the fall of 2016, he was named captain of the North American team that was set to play in the World Cup of Hockey in Toronto.

The best young players in North America were selected for the under-23 team. It was something of a reunion for Connor, and he was looking forward to seeing so many of his friends again. "The Canadian guys are pretty familiar with each other, having grown up through the system together," he said.

This young team was a new concept for the World Cup. A lot of people didn't think they stood a chance against the "men" of hockey, like Sidney Crosby and Alex Ovechkin. Team North America started the tournament with a game against Finland on September 18, 2016. Under Connor's leadership, North America beat Finland 4–1. Connor picked up an assist and displayed some crafty moves.

Next up was Russia. Again Connor picked up an assist, breaking open and giving Auston Matthews a pretty set up at the side of the net. The move stunned the crowd. But it was a tough, hard-skating game and they ultimately lost the battle 4–3.

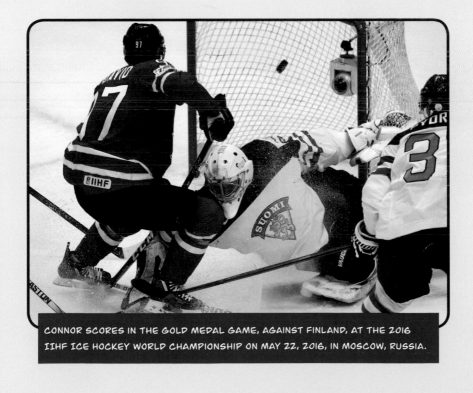

CONNOR SCORES IN THE GOLD MEDAL GAME, AGAINST FINLAND, AT THE 2016 IIHF ICE HOCKEY WORLD CHAMPIONSHIP ON MAY 22, 2016, IN MOSCOW, RUSSIA.

In their third contest, North America fought against the skilled Swedish team in a back-and-forth match. Team North America pushed by the Swedes in overtime, and Connor picked up yet another beautiful assist.

When the news came that North America wouldn't advance to the semifinals, fans were crushed. Team North America had a 2–1 record, but so did Russia. Because Connor's team had lost to the Russians in round-robin play, Team Russia was the one to advance. But Team North America had become the fan favourite. Dynamic young players like Connor had dazzled the crowd.

AFTER CONNOR MOVED TO ERIE, WHO CALLED AND GAVE HIM A PEP TALK?

WAYNE GRETZKY!

SOPHOMORE SUPERSTAR

Before the start of his second year in the NHL, the Oilers were considering a bold move — making Connor captain. This would make him the youngest captain in NHL history. Many experts thought that the pressure might be too much for him. He was so young! Why not let him play for another year?

But when Connor met with the coaches, he assured them he was ready for the role. Oilers coach Todd McLellan explained their decision to the media, saying, "He's mature beyond his years . . . he's dealt with all of you since he was foutreen. He handles himself very well and takes care of his teammates."

Connor was thrilled to have been named captain and was excited to lead his team. He had great confidence in his alternate captains: Jordan Eberle and Ryan Nugent-Hopkins had played a few seasons with the Oilers already, and Milan Lucic had won the Stanley Cup. When the four young captains were presented to the media days before the Oilers' home opener, they walked out of the dressing room side by side. The media swarmed them. Connor smiled and answered their questions. He wanted this job. He knew he could do it . . . and he couldn't wait to prove it.

MAKING HIS MARK

In his second season in the NHL, Connor didn't miss a single game. The Oilers' last game of the season was April 9, against the Vancouver Canucks. He went into that game with 98 points. Was it possible to reach the 100-point milestone?

A beautiful pass to Drake Caggiula after Connor managed to thread the puck through an obstacle course of Canucks brought him to point 99. Caggiula had popped the puck in from the side of the net, making the score 3–1 for the Oilers in the second period.

The anticipation quickly built in the stands. The crowd started cheering for Connor — he only needed one more point! When the third period started, they held their breath. But not for long! Just 1:50 into the third period, Connor passed the puck to his linemate Leon Draisaitl, who snapped it past the Canucks goalie.

The fans in Rogers Place leapt to their feet, cheering and chanting, "MVP . . . MVP . . . MVP." They cheered so loudly that the Oilers players couldn't hear head coach Todd McLellan talking to them on the bench.

After the goal, Caggiula picked up the puck and brought it to the bench. Connor's teammates wrapped tape around the puck, wrote "100 points" on it and gave it to him as a souvenir. With 30 goals and 70 assists, Connor was just the eighth Edmonton Oiler to score 100 points in one season.

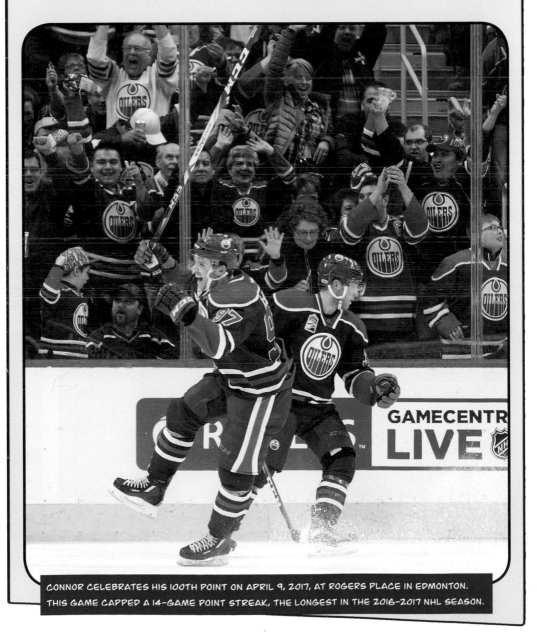

CONNOR CELEBRATES HIS 100TH POINT ON APRIL 9, 2017, AT ROGERS PLACE IN EDMONTON. THIS GAME CAPPED A 14-GAME POINT STREAK, THE LONGEST IN THE 2016-2017 NHL SEASON.

The regular season ended on April 9, 2017. It was official — Connor McDavid had won the Art Ross Trophy as the NHL's points leader. He had even beaten his childhood hero Sidney Crosby! And for the first time in more than a decade, the Oilers had made it to the Stanley Cup playoffs. Just like when he was captain of the Erie Otters, the NHL's youngest captain led his team — which some were now calling "Connor McDavid and the Edmonton Oilers" — to the playoffs.

PLAYOFF ROLLER COASTER

This would be Connor's first NHL playoff experience, and his team was to meet the San Jose Sharks in the first round. The city of Edmonton was going crazy, buying orange T-shirts and pompoms, and even more orange jerseys with "McDavid" stitched on the back. Billboards with Connor's face on them were put up all over the city. When Connor stepped on the ice for his first playoff game, he couldn't believe how excited the fans were, how they yelled and cheered and waved their signs and pompoms.

Every single shift Connor was on the ice, he had big players covering him. He had to use his speed to get by them. The first game went to overtime and the Oilers lost 3–2. It was discouraging, but Connor regrouped his team in the dressing room before the next game and the Oilers came on strong in game two to win 2–0. Connor and his teammates kept pushing and scoring. They won their first series in six games, with Connor scoring two goals and earning two assists.

In the next round, the Oilers faced off against the Anaheim Ducks, who had just swept the Calgary Flames. It was an absolute battle of a seven-game series, with two games going into nail-biting overtime action. In game 5, the Oilers had a 3–0 lead and with 15 seconds left on the clock, the Ducks tied the game on a controversial goal . . . and then won in double OT.

Ultimately, the Oilers were not able to best their division rivals. But they had made significant gains with their young captain at the helm.

"We took a huge step forward," Connor said. "If we'd have told you we'd go seven in the second series, back in September, I don't think anyone would have believed it. We'll be back."

On June 21, 2017, at the NHL Awards ceremony in Las Vegas, Connor was a big winner. He won the Hart Memorial Trophy, awarded to the player judged most valuable to his team, and the Ted Lindsay Award for

Most Valuable Player as voted by the players. After accepting his Ted Lindsay Award, Connor stood at the microphone and, like the team-focused captain he is, said, "To my teammates, I owe it all to you guys. Honestly it means the world to play with you guys each and every night. I love you guys." These two awards were in addition to the Art Ross Trophy — Connor had finished his second year in the NHL with an award hat trick!

At the ceremony, Connor was also named the cover athelete for the EA Sports *NHL 18* video game, recognizing that this young star and his dynamic style of play are the face of hockey's future. Through hard work, dedication and perseverance, Connor McDavid has proven he is a force to be reckoned with in the NHL, now and for years to come.